A·FIRST·BOOK·OF
COUNTING

A·FIRST·BOOK·OF
COUNTING

Illustrated by David Anstey
Written by A J Wood

MODERN PUBLISHING
A Division of Unisystems, Inc.
New York, New York 10022

1

One dinosaur watched...

...two
dinosaurs
dancing.

3

Three
dinosaurs
saw...

...four
dinosaurs
falling.

Five
dinosaurs
found...

...six
dinosaurs
singing.

Seven
dinosaurs
saw...

...eight
dinosaurs
eating.

Nine
dinosaurs
woke...

...ten
dinosaurs
sleeping.

The End